Presented to: Bo
From: Margot with love
On the Occasion of: Holy Week '82 & our struggle "to strike or not to strike."

The Lord is my keeper.
— Hebrews 13:6

The Beauty of Caring

LLOYD JOHN OGILVIE

The Beauty of Caring

HARVEST HOUSE PUBLISHERS
Eugene, Oregon 97402

The Beauty of Caring

Copyright © 1981 by Harvest House Publishers
Eugene, Oregon 97402

Library of Congress Catalog Card Number 80-80464
ISBN 0-89081-244-6

All rights reserved. No portion of this book may be reproduced in any form without written permission of the Publisher.

Printed in the United States of America.

Design by Koechel/Peterson Design
Minneapolis, Minnesota 55406

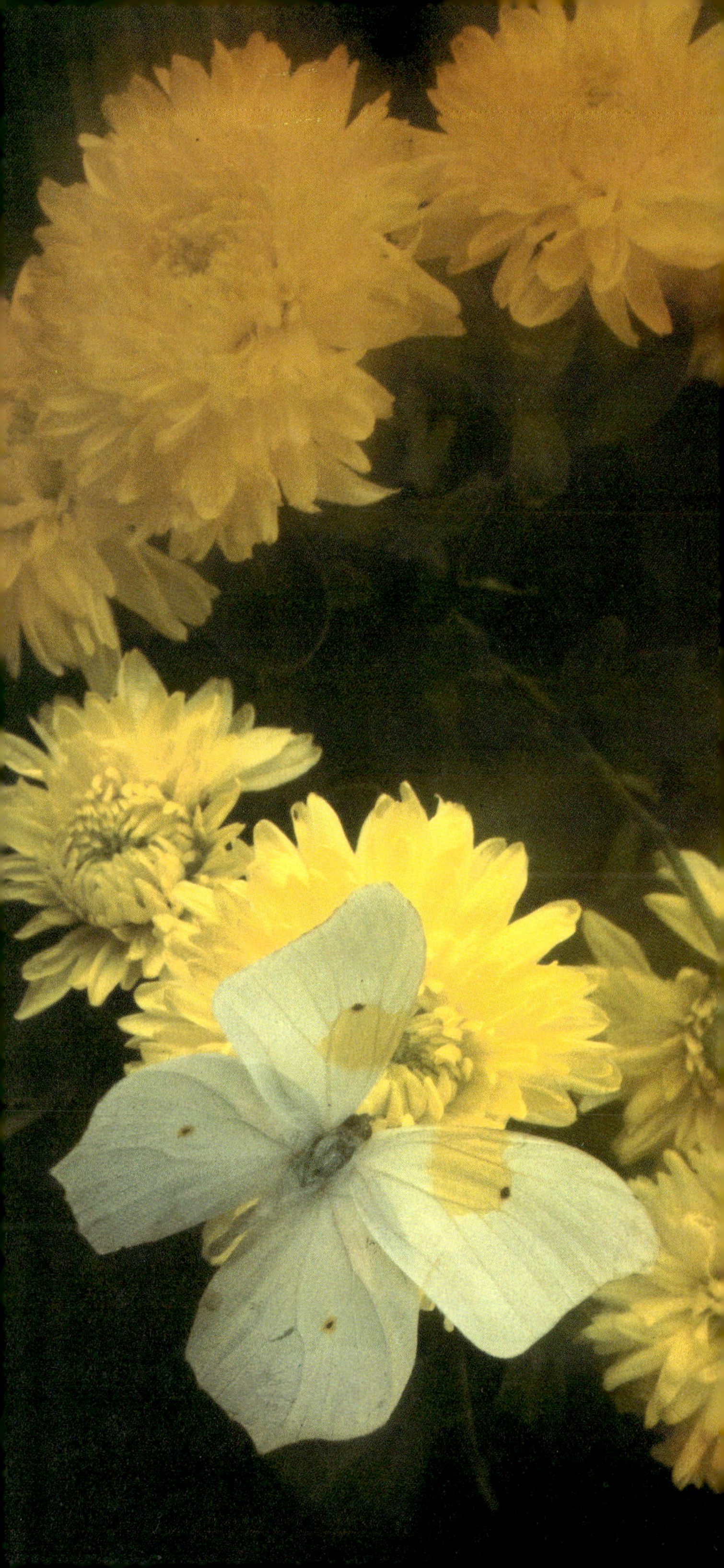

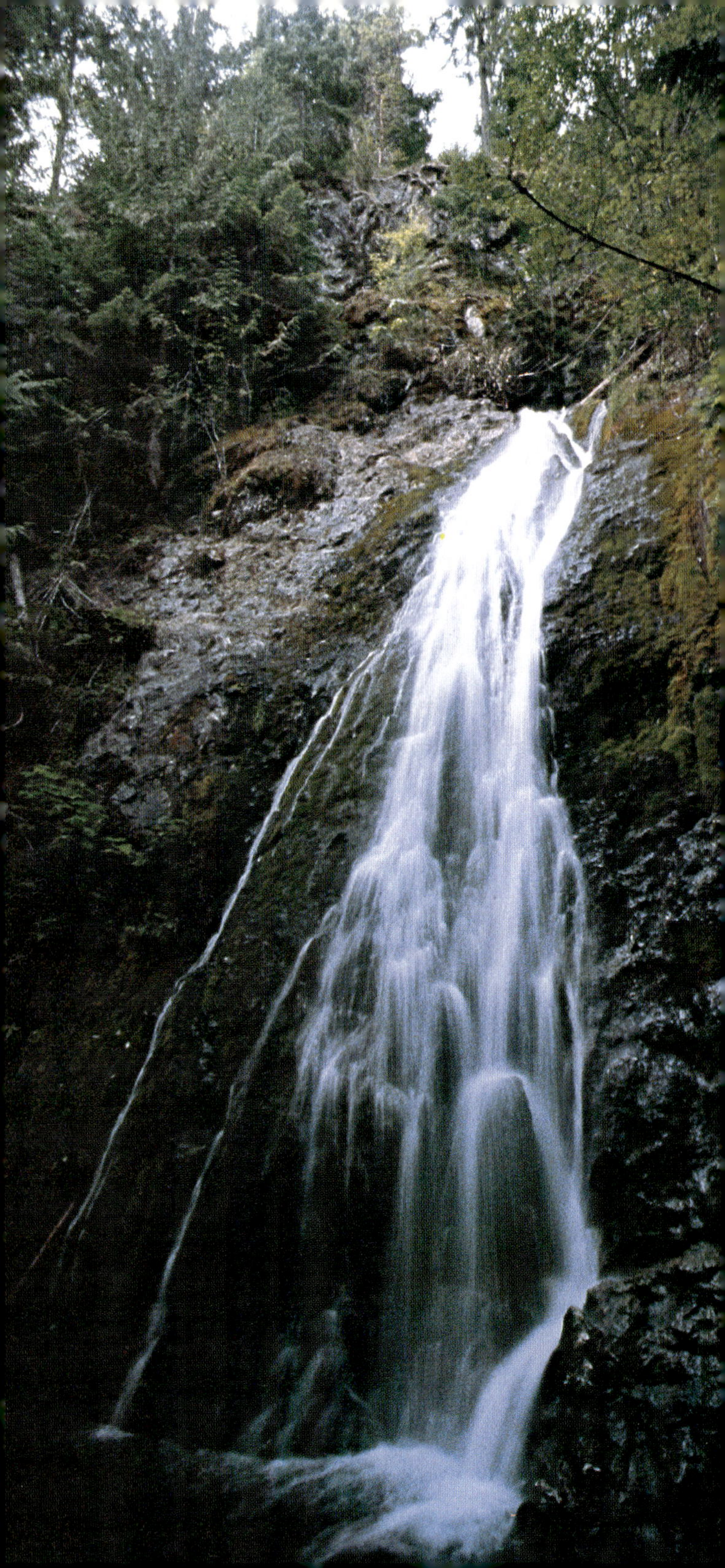

I Know How You Feel

"I prayed to God that He would baptize my heart into the sense of all conditions, so that I might be able to enter into the needs and sorrows of all."

George Fox

"If someone who is supposed to be a Christian has money enough to live well, and sees a brother in need and won't help him—how can God's love be within him?"

I John 3:17, TLB

"Man may dismiss compassion from his heart, but God will never."

William Cowper

Caring and compassion are inseparable. The Latin word for compassion is a combination of *com*, together, and *pati*, to feel or suffer. It means to feel together, as well as for, another person.

The conversion of our feelings is a vital part of becoming dynamic Christians. Life, with its disappointments and hurts, can harden our feelings. We learn how to protect, guard, even hide our true feelings. When Christ begins His transforming work in us, He not only reorients our minds around His lordship, but makes us feeling persons again. He helps us to get in touch with our feelings.

The fact of the Gospel engenders faith, and faith releases our feelings. The result is that we are able to feel what's happening to the people around us. Compassion is caring in action. Our care about how people feel must be expressed in some action, a giving of ourselves and our resources, as a tangible expression of our feelings. The words "I know how you feel" communicate comfort and oneness. Then proof that we really know comes when we step into action to actually help lift the burden. Who needs that from you today?

"I Couldn't Care Less!"

The popular slang saying can be taken two ways: it can be an angry expression that we do not care or a profound commitment to care.

So often when we say, "I couldn't care less!" we have been hurt deeply. Something which has been said or done has put a tourniquet on our hearts, cutting off the flow of concern. It is a clumsy use of negatives to try to say that we have reached the ultimate level of not caring. But if that were the case, we wouldn't have to protest so vehemently. Actually, what we are saying is, "I wish I didn't care so much!"

Now consider a very different way of using this expression. When we witness to how much Christ cares for us, the lengths He went to on the cross, the unmerited grace He offers us, the forgiveness He gives before we ask, then we must say, "I dare not care less!"

Who's on Your Agenda?

So often before a meeting someone will ask, "What's on the agenda?" There's a much more important question we all need to ask: "Who's on your agenda?" But even that is not the most crucial question for a caring person. The great need is to ask, "Who's on the Lord's agenda for me?" We can't care for everyone. There are not enough hours in the day to meet all the people concerns which confront us.

Often when we open ourselves to become caring, we are engulfed by the sea of human needs and the opportunities to serve. We will go under if we try to answer every call for help. The great need is to ask the Lord to give us discernment about the specific people He's put on our particular agenda.

He will guide us in the stewardship of our resources of time, energy and money. God's work, done with His direction, in His strength, will be effective and lasting. When we know the who, what and when of guided caring, we will feel the power of cooperating with the Lord.

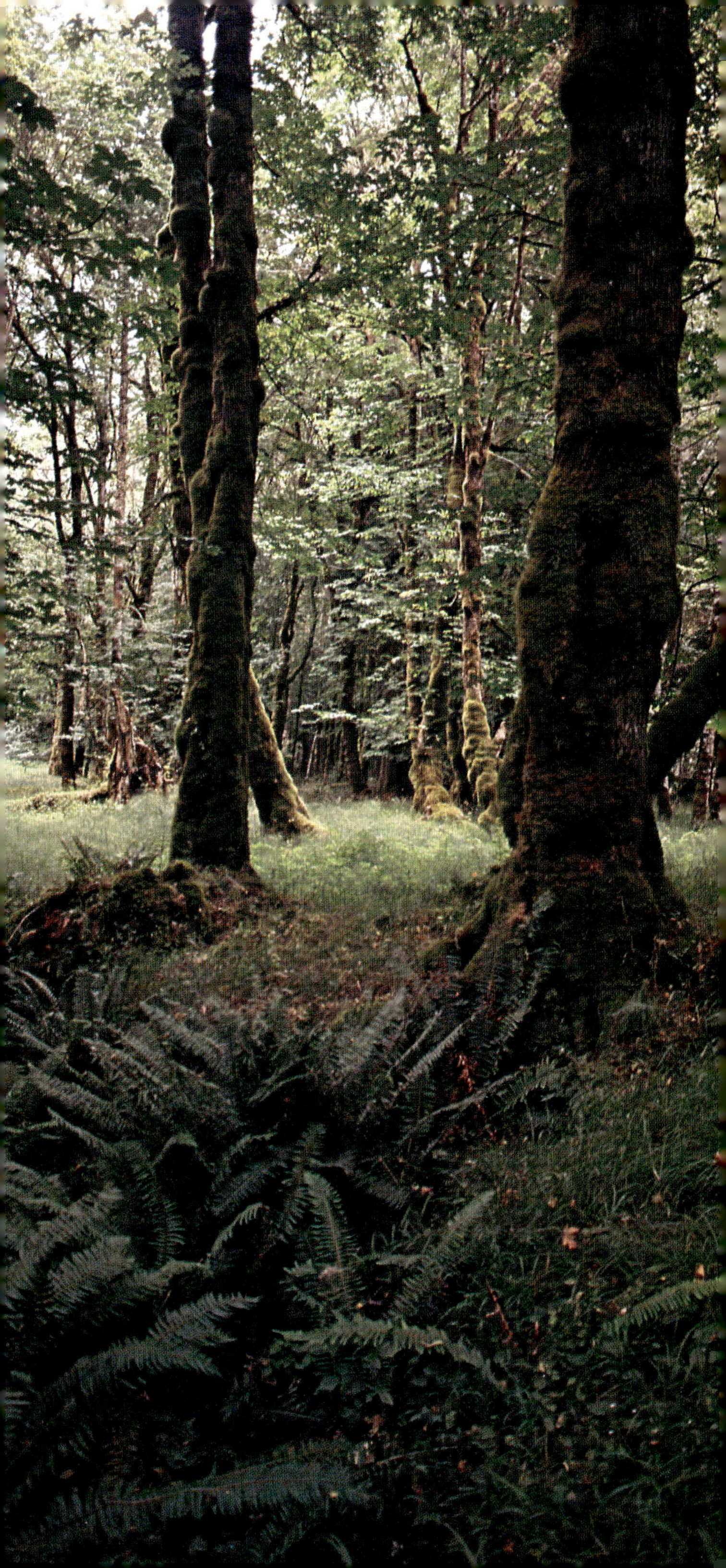

Let People Care for You

A dynamic expression of caring is to be able to receive caring. Let people love you! But that means to be vulnerable. People cannot care about us if they do not know our needs. We give people a special gift when we become honest and open about what's happening to and around us. Independence and self-reliance block deep caring. A person who refuses to be cared for by others will usually end up caring little about the people around him.

Share your needs, ask for others' prayers, seek their insight and wisdom. Your openness will create an openness in the people you want to help. It takes a lot of energy to keep the facade of adequacy. The mask brings strained relationships. People feel put down and guilty in the presence of a person who pretends to "have it all together."

We begin to become caring persons when we let God care for us. Then our hearts are set on fire with care for others. But the "I'm going to care for you!" attitude often sets up resistance in the very people about whom we care. Asking them for their care for you is often the first step in preparing an openness for you to care for them.

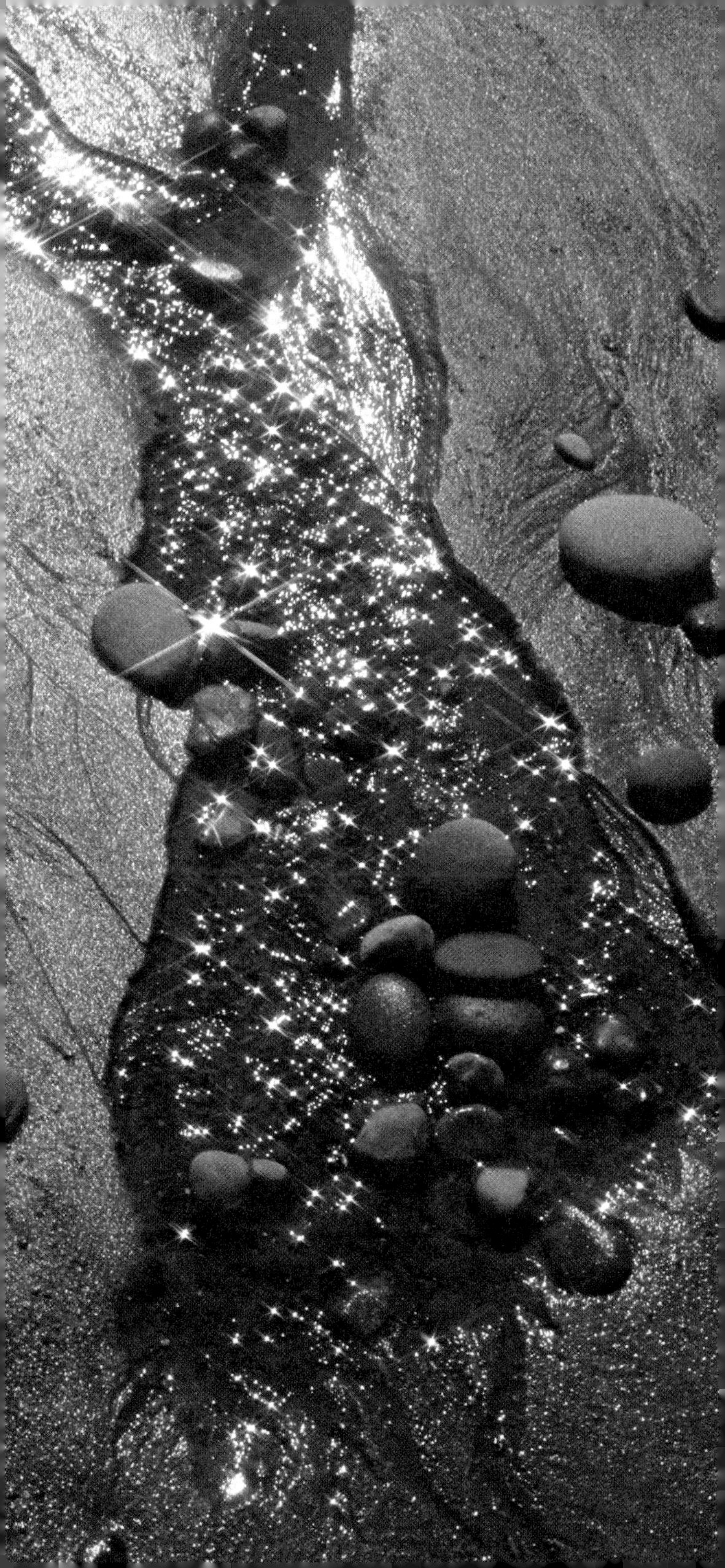

Caring Begins With Enjoying People

"There is no one like Timothy for having a real interest in you; everyone else seems to be worrying about his own plans and not those of Jesus Christ."

Philippians 2:20-21, TLB

"I want to remind you to stir into flame the strength and boldness that is in you.... For the Holy Spirit, God's gift, does not want you to be afraid of people, but to be wise and strong, and love them and enjoy being with them."

II Timothy 1:6-7, TLB

It is interesting to note the advice Paul gave to Timothy and what he said to the Philippians about his faithful friend. The young man lived out what the Apostle encouraged him to express as a caring person. He had an interest in people. Christ's plans were more important than his own. That's quite a compliment; and yet, why should it be so unusual? The one thing the world should be able to expect from us is that we are interested in people and enjoy being with them.

We often look around for spectacular ways of caring for people. Enjoying them is a first step. When people feel that, they will welcome our insight into their needs and our practical help. We need two conversions: one to Christ and the other to people. The first gives us the power for the second. Conversion means to turn around, a U-turn from self-centeredness to Christ-centeredness and then to His plans for us with people. Can what Paul said about Timothy be said of you?

Does God Really Care?

"Thou hast made me drink
of the wine of astonishment."

Psalm 60:3, NKJV

"When I consider Thy heavens,
the work of Thy fingers,
The moon and the stars, which
Thou hast ordained;
What is man, that Thou dost
take thought of him?
And the son of man, that Thou
dost care for him?
Yet Thou hast made him a
little lower than God,
And dost crown him with
glory and majesty!"

Psalm 8:3-5, NASB

No wonder the Psalmist was astonished. W. H. Davies said, "What is life if, full of care, we have no time to stand and stare?" The personalized caring of God is the only antidote to our cares. Rodin, the famous sculptor, said about the barrenness of the arts in his time, "My friends have lost the art of admiration."

Astonished admiration grows in us when we realize that God knows all about us. A sense of wonder grows in us when we consider that it would take a car racing at top speed nine years to reach the moon; three hundred years to reach the sun; eight thousand, three hundred years to reach the planet Neptune; seventy-five million years to reach Alpha Centauri; and seven hundred million years to reach the Pole Star.

And yet God has created us a little lower than Himself so that we can know Him, experience His love, and trust His caring providence in our needs.

Think Magnificently of God

"First of all, my child, think magnificently of God. Magnify His providence; adore His power; pray to Him frequently and incessantly. Bear Him always in your mind; teach your thoughts to reverence Him in every place, for there is no place where He is not. Therefore, my child, fear and worship, and love God; first and last, think magnificently of God."

Paternus to his son

A caring person has learned to think magnificently of God. We cannot give away what we do not have. The more God's care for us is the focus of our minds and hearts, the more, almost inadvertently, we will care for others. Contemplation of the greatness of God and a constant experience of His majesty and His immanence will produce a life built on the foundation of compassion.

"As the marsh-hen secretly builds
 on the watery sod,
Behold I will build me a nest
 on the greatness of God:

...

"By so many roots as the marsh grass
 sends in the sod,
I will heartily lay me a-hold
 on the greatness of God...."
  Sidney Lanier, "The Marshes of Glynn"

Who Is My Neighbor?

"'A certain man went down from Jerusalem to Jericho, and fell among thieves, who stripped him of his clothing, wounded him, and departed, leaving him half dead. And by chance a certain priest came down that road. And when he saw him, he passed by on the other side. And likewise a Levite, when he was at the place, came and looked at him, and passed by on the other side.

"'But a certain Samaritan, as he journeyed, came where he was. And when he saw him, he had compassion on him, and went to him and bandaged his wounds, pouring on oil and wine; and he set him on his own donkey, brought him to an inn, and took care of him. And the next day, when he departed, he took out two denarii, gave them to the innkeeper, and said to him, "Take care of him; and whatever more you spend, when I come again, I will repay you." 'Now which of these do you think was neighbor to him who fell among the thieves?' ...Then [Jesus] said..., 'Go and do likewise.'"

Luke 10:30-37, NKJV

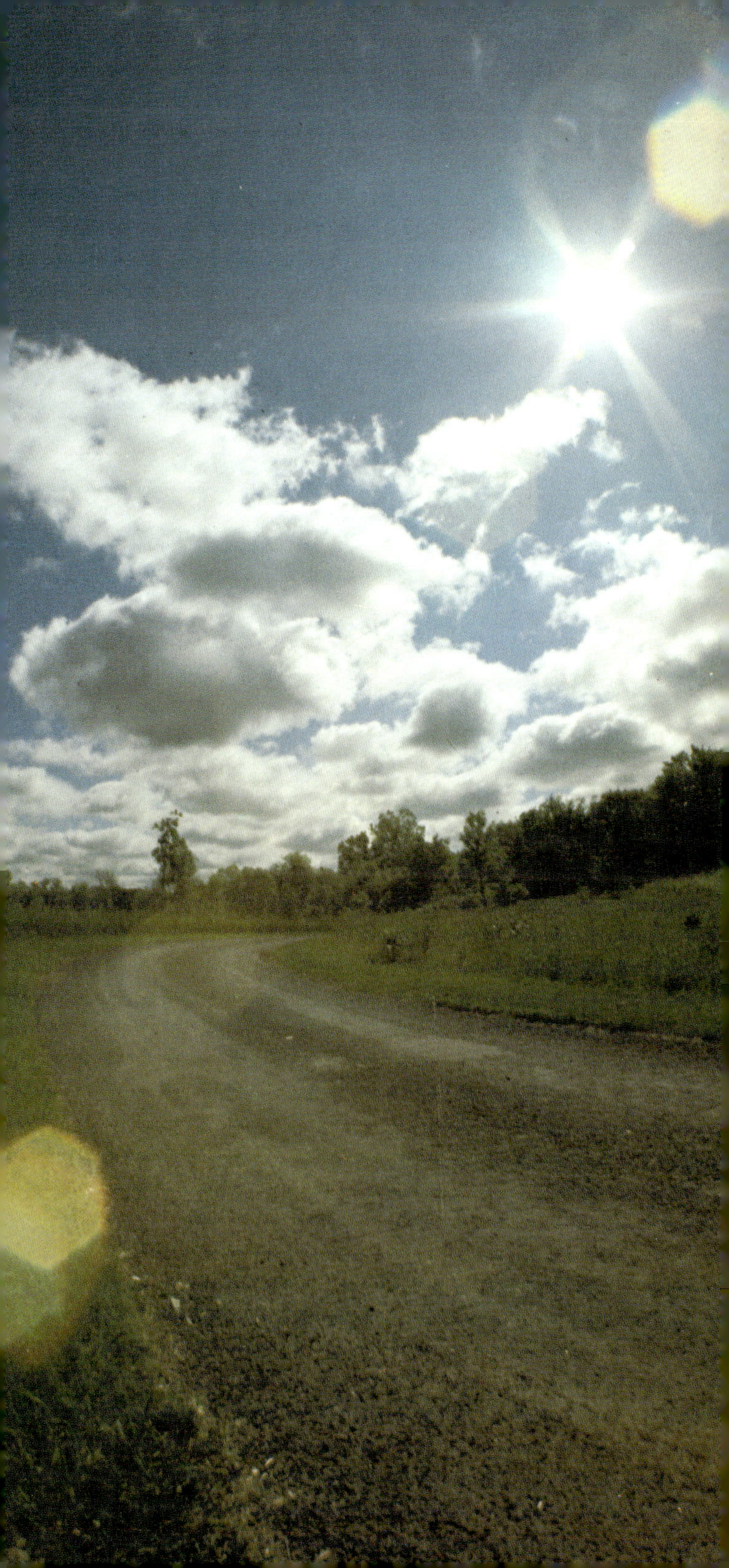

Spontaneous Caring

The parable of the Good Samaritan calls us to spontaneous caring. The key phrase is "and by chance." The Greek word translated by the word "chance" means coincidence. But not even that word gets at the core of the meaning of the Greek word. Actually, it means a confluence of circumstances which seem to happen by chance but are really events interwoven by Divine Providence for the accomplishment of a greater purpose.

None of the three men who came upon the wounded traveler had planned ahead for the opportunity of caring. The two religious leaders passed by the beaten man because of rules and regulations. Perhaps they supposed him dead. To touch a dead body would have made them ceremonially unclean for twenty-four hours. We wonder if they were rushing to the temple services that day.

But did the man make no groans of pain? Try as we will, our efforts to excuse the priest and the Levite do not hold true to the caring God whom they would worship in the temple. Their problem was that they lacked spontaneous caring, an immediate response to unexpected need.

The Samaritans were hated by the Jews, and yet it was a Samaritan whom Jesus exemplified as a caring neighbor. His plans, schedule, privacy and the danger of being attacked by the very robbers who had beaten the wounded man did not dissuade the Samaritan. He cared for him personally and then paid the innkeeper to care for him until he returned.

God does not cause the tragedies of human needs, but He does use them as opportunities for us to cooperate with Him. Stop praying and the coincidences stop happening. Our task is to be prepared for what life prepares. Jesus was sublimely interruptable and ready to respond.

To Hear and Do!

"Whoever hears these sayings of Mine, and does them, I will liken him to a wise man who built his house on the rock: and the rain descended, the floods came, and the winds blew and beat on that house; and it did not fall, for it was founded on the rock."

Matthew 7:24-25, NKJV

Jesus ended the Sermon on the Mount with an investiture into the invincible. He called His disciples to live an authentic life in which hearing and doing were part of one experience. The authority He had would be given to the disciples. Life built on a solid rock would be the confirmation of receptivity and responsibility.

The thing that astonished people about Jesus was not only what He said but what He did. He didn't just talk about power; He did mighty works. He not only preached sacrificial love, He went to the cross. We will astonish people by what Christ means to us not only by what we say but by what we are—exemplified in what we do in caring.

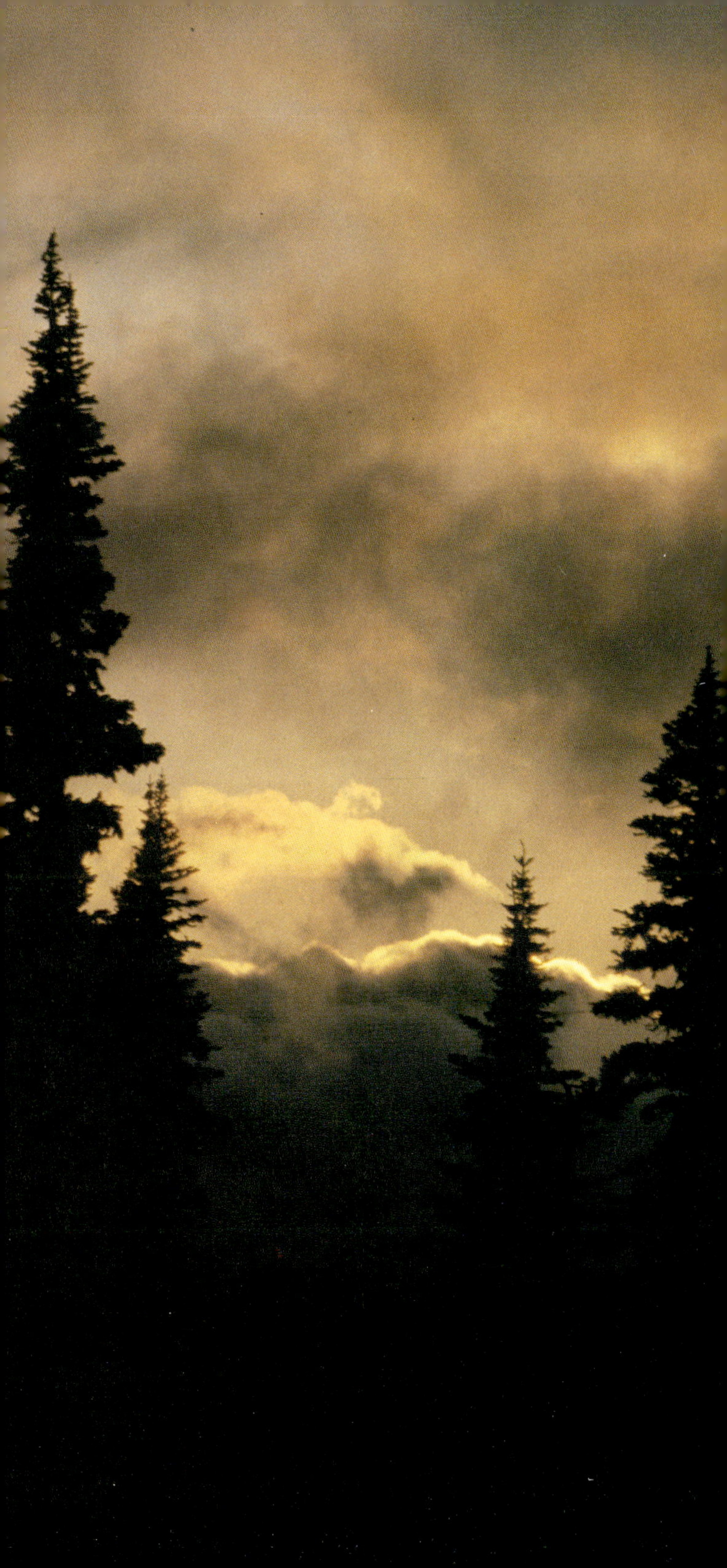

We belong to Christ. The awesome authority He had over suffering, sin and sickness is entrusted to us. We are not powerless victims. We have been sent on a mission with the assurance of unlimited supply lines. I once asked a general why he had been so successful. His answer is a good motto for a person who is called to care for others. "I knew that ultimately we would win. I never underestimated my enemy, and I kept my supply lines open."

I will never forget the words of my professor, James Stewart of Edinburgh, Scotland. I think of them often when I need to reclarify my purpose and power as one called to care.

"The life which flows from Christ into a man is something different, not only in degree but also in kind. It is a new quality. There is a new creation, not just an intensification of powers already possessed, but the sudden emergence of an entirely new and original element whenever a man comes to be in Christ. He begins to live in the sphere of the post-resurrection life in Jesus."

That's the source of our authority to live an astonishing life!

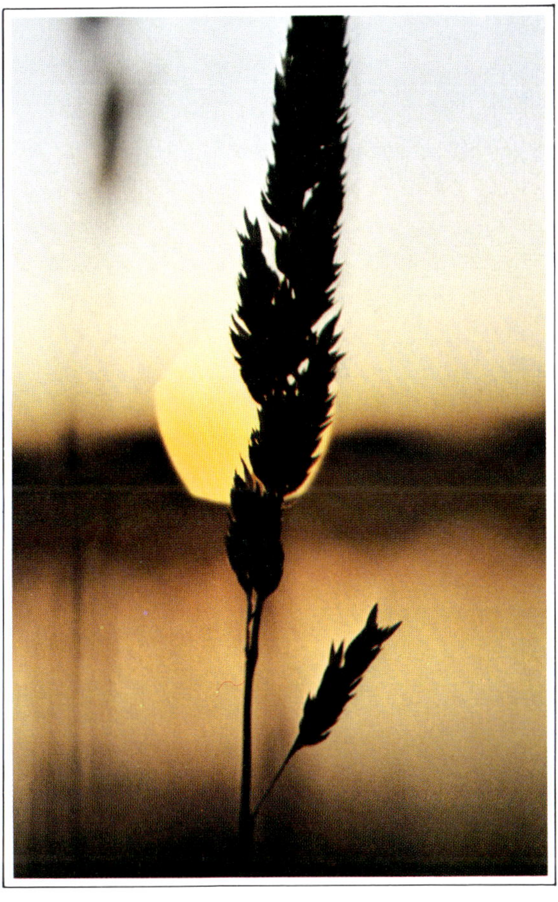

Millionth-Mile Living

"You have heard that it has been said, 'An eye for an eye and a tooth for a tooth.' But I tell you not to resist an evil person. But whoever slaps you on your right cheek, turn the other to him also. And if anyone wants to sue you and take away your tunic, let him have your cloak also. And whoever shall compel you to go one mile, go with him two. Give to him who asks you, and from him who wants to borrow from you do not turn away."

Matthew 5:38-42, NKJV

Really caring means millionth-mile living. In the Sermon on the Mount, Jesus gives us a radical challenge for remedial caring. His people were very proud of their distinctive application of the lextalionis, the practice of exact retribution. It had brought sanity into the measurement of what a person could do to someone who had harmed or hurt him. Jesus outdistanced that practice by a million miles; He called for no retribution at all! No longer was there to be an-eye-for-an-eye, tooth-for-a-tooth retaliation.

The Master went way beyond the quid pro quo of equal expression of anger and resentment. He drives that home with three very pointed illustrations: turning your right cheek toward your assailant after the left one has been given a blow by the palm of his right hand, giving a person who sues you for your tunic your only cloak, and going the second mile for someone who compels you to go one. The Romans flaunted their authority to conscript a citizen of a captured territory to carry a load. Imagine a follower of the Master saying to a Roman soldier, "I've finished my mile. Can't I help you by going on farther?"

The Lord exemplified going not one extra mile but limitless miles of caring, concern, forgiveness and willingness to help others. His cross is our mandate and motivation for that. The only way to live millionth-mile caring is by His power. The life He challenges us to live can be accomplished only when He lives in us. As we assume the burden of caring for others, He says,

"Come to me, all you who labor and are heavy laden, and I will give you rest."
                                              Matthew 11:28

Interruptable

"We must be ready to allow ourselves to be interrupted by God. God will be constantly crossing our paths and canceling our plans by sending us people claims and petitions. We may pass them by, preoccupied with more important tasks.... When we do that, we pass by the visible sign of the cross raised in our path to show us that, not our way, but God's way must be done. It is a strange fact that Christians frequently consider their work so important and urgent that they will allow nothing to disturb them. They think they are doing God a service in this, but actually they are disdaining God's 'crooked yet straight path.' But it is a part of the discipline of humility that we must not spare our hand where it can perform a service and that we do not assume that our schedule is our own to manage, but allow it to be arranged by God."

Dietrich Bonhoeffer, *Life Together*

We will never be free to be truly caring persons until we accept interruptions as gifts from God. We will fret and fume until we welcome the intrusions as the Lord Himself coming to us in people's needs.

There's a lovely story of a little boy who got his fist caught in a valuable vase. His family tried in vain to pull it off. The family doctor was called. When he arrived, he said there was nothing to do but break the vase. When he did, it was discovered that the little boy was clutching a penny. If he had let go, his fist would have been relaxed and easily removed. Clutching our schedules and plans is like that. Let go and let God interrupt you!

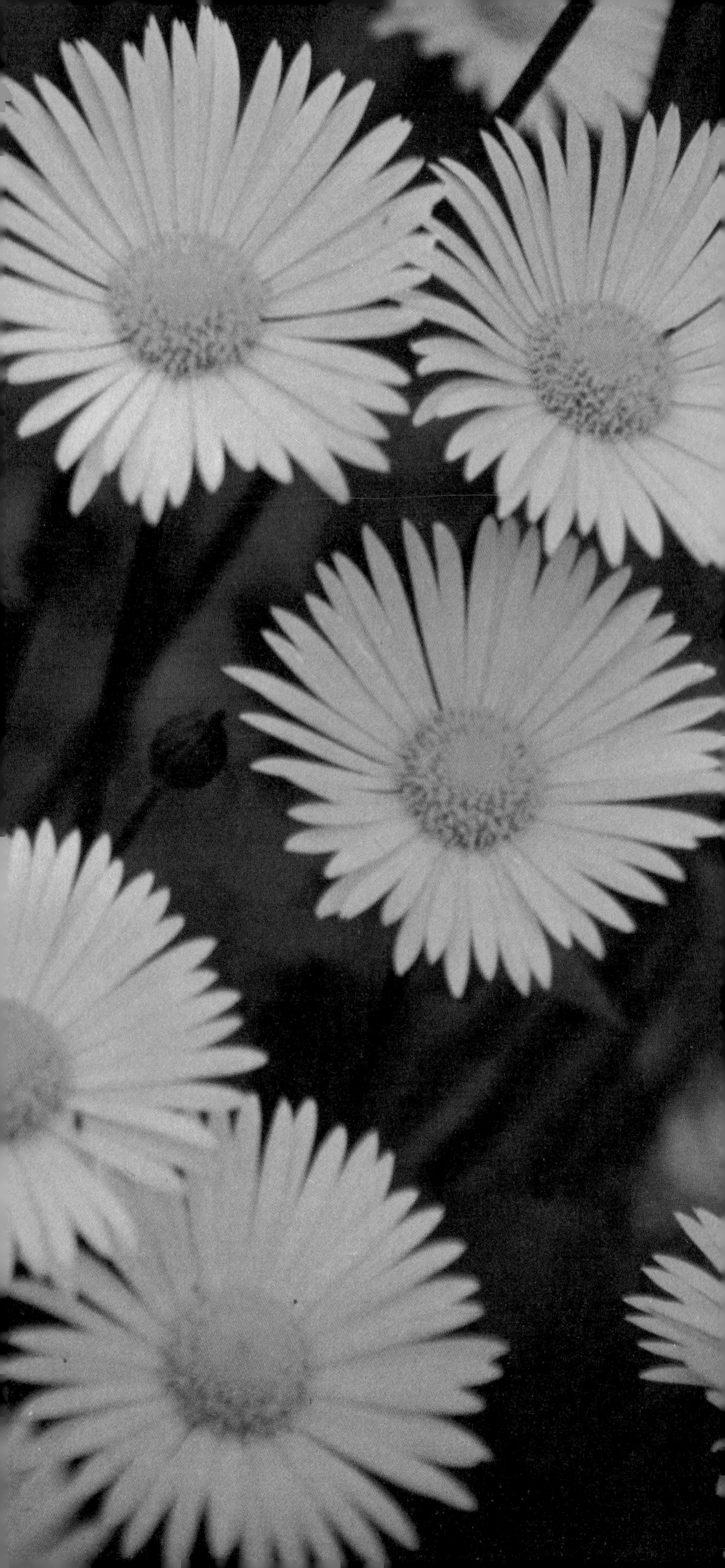

Called to Be Servants

"Jesus, knowing that the Father had given all things into His hands, and that He had come from God and was going to God, rose from supper, laid aside His garments, took a towel, and girded Himself. After that, He poured water into a basin and began to wash the disciples' feet...."

John 13:3-5, NKJV

The disciples were alarmed when they arrived at the upper room where they were to celebrate the Passover with the Master. Someone was missing! They looked at one another with embarrassed glances. How could their host who had granted the use of the room there in Jerusalem have been so insensitive? There was no servant to wash their feet. Who would do it?

No wonder they were shocked when Jesus took the role of the servant and washed their feet. Peter objected. He was clever enough to know that if the Master washed his feet, he would have to wash other feet. Jesus became the servant to help the disciples discover that He had called them to serve the world in His name.

Note that Jesus took the towel and basin because He knew that He had come from God and was going to God. When we know that we belong to God and our ultimate destiny is in Him, we can accept our calling to give ourselves away. Nothing else counts except knowing and doing what pleases Him. If our destiny and destination are settled, we can give ourselves away with abandonment. We don't need to save ourselves. The more we give away, the more we receive.

The symbols of a caring person are a towel and basin. To wash people's feet means to become their servants to help in whatever ways we can. We can experience great freedom and joy when we think of our lives, work and relationships as opportunities to serve. Jesus said,

"For I have given you an example, that you should do as I have done to you. Most assuredly, I say to you, a servant is not greater than his master; nor is he who is sent greater than he who sent him. If you know these things, happy are you if you do them."

John 13:15-17, NKJV

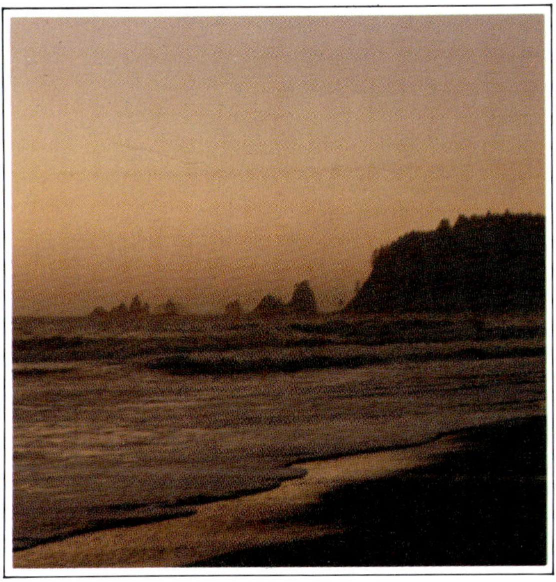

Dare to Be Specific

"A Christian is the most free lord of all, and subject to none; a Christian is the most dutiful servant of all, and subject to everyone."

Martin Luther

Called to be servants, yes, but how? What does it mean in specific terms to wash another person's feet? For me it means five things, all beginning with an *i*:

1. We are *impelled*. It is not just the needs of people but the needs in our own lives which Christ has met that impel us to want to help others as we have been helped.

2. We are to *identify*. A servant does not serve at a safe distance; he feels the pain and suffering of another as if it were his own. When God came in Christ, He did not give lofty advice; He became one of us!

3. We *intercede*. Prayers of intervention not only unleash the power of God in another person's life but also give us clarity about what the Lord wants us to say to that person. The intensity of our caring must be focused so that it meets the deepest need.

4. A servant becomes *involved*. That means listening to a person and actually daring to enter his or her situation. It is so easy to tell a person what to do with a problem but much more difficult to get inside his or her skin and feel the anguish, fear or frustration. People need an intense "I'm with you, I understand!" empathy.

5. We are meant to be *incisive* in introducing people to the Savior. We do not care profoundly if we help people with physical or emotional suffering but leave them with an eternal problem, their relationship with Christ. A servant earns the right to be heard by caring. We are warned through Jeremiah not to heal the wound superficially. We dare not say, "Peace, peace!" when there is no peace. If we care for people, we will find an opportunity to tell them why we care and then tell them about the One who cares a million times more than we do.

Admit, Submit, Commit, Transmit

"We make a living by what we get, but we make a life by what we give."
Winston S. Churchill

"He who sees a need and waits to be asked for help is as unkind as if he had refused it."
Dante

"The worst sin toward our fellow creatures is not to hate them, but to be indifferent to them."
George Bernard Shaw

Samuel Wilberforce gave us a four-step plan for becoming caring persons. He said, "Christianity can be condensed into four words: admit, submit, commit and transmit." When the needs of people and the world around us break our hearts, we can admit to our lack of caring. Then we can submit to Christ's command to love one another.

That is followed by a commitment of our total lives to Him. We have been loved and forgiven to prepare us to join the Lord in a ministry of caring. Then, filled with His loving Spirit, we can transmit what has been given to us to others. The final step of any learning is action. The litmus test of realized truth is to determine the extent of our remedial behavior.

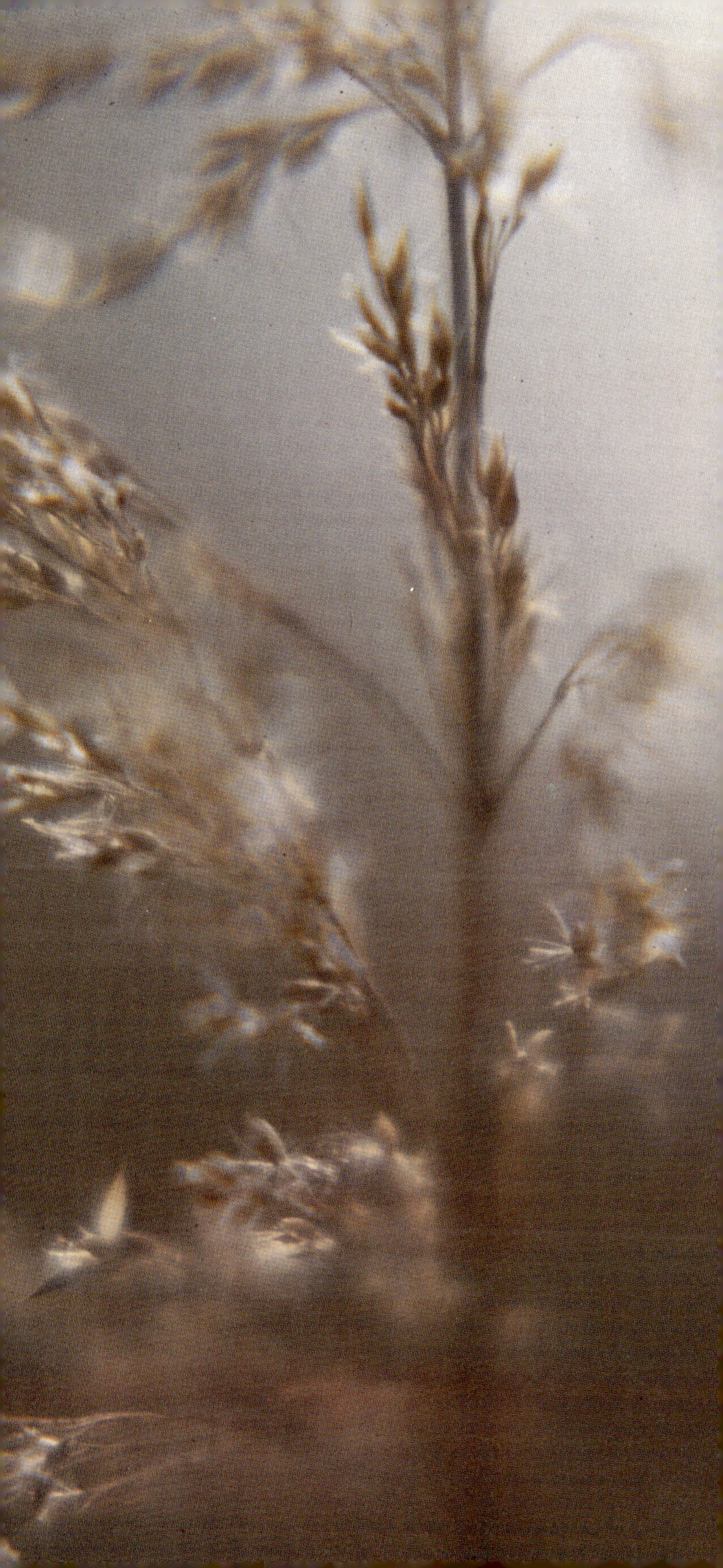

The Day God Cried

"And when He had come near, He saw the city and wept over it...."

Luke 19:41, NKJV

Really caring often brings us to tears. We are not alone when our hearts break. Jesus cried over Jerusalem when He looked down on the city during the Triumphal Entry. Remember who He was—and is! The Messiah was none other than God with us. It was God who cried on that day we celebrate as Palm Sunday.

What Jesus said as He sobbed tells us why. The people did not know the things which belonged to their true peace. They were missing the time of Divine visitation. So do we when He comes to us with the opportunity of caring for someone. The motive for concern is that He's cried over us. What have we done or failed to do that makes our Lord weep over us? When we identify that and experience His passion for us on the cross, we become passionate to care as He has cared about us. We share the heart of God when we know the anguish of tears for another person.

His tears for us soften the hard clay of our hearts so we can be molded in His image. Our rigid, hard judgmentalism or aloof carelessness will be turned into words and action for the needs of others. Jesus not only cried over His people, He went to the cross for them — and for you and me!

Resurrection Caring

One of my favorite poems is John Masefield's "The Everlasting Mercy."[*] It is about how Saul Kane, a brutal, heartless man, was found by God and discovered in His mercy the motive of a caring life. His experience of the resurrection made him part of the caring Easter people all the year through.

"O glory of the lighted mind.
How dead I'd been, how dumb, how blind.
The station brook, to my new eyes,
Was babbling out of Paradise,
The waters rushing from the rain
Were singing Christ was risen again.
I thought all earthly creatures knelt
From rapture of the joy I felt."

Now see the implications of the resurrection in Saul Kane's heart for a new quality of caring about others.

"The prison doors had broken in
And I knew that I was done with sin.
I knew that Christ had given me birth
To brother all the souls on earth."

---

[*] Copyright 1911. John Masefield, "The Everlasting Mercy," The MacMillan Co.

Rebirth is a recall to caring. When the stone of indifference is rolled away and we are raised to new life with Christ, our urgent desire is to brother and sister all the souls on earth. A sure sign that we have accepted Christ's resurrection is that we have experienced our own, and the authentic test of that is in ascertaining whether or not we have Christ's indwelling Spirit of caring.

Wait for the Lord

"Those who wait for the Lord will gain new strength; they will mount up with wings like eagles, they will run and not get tired, they will walk and not become weary."

Isaiah 40:31

This often-quoted verse is understood only if we read and accept the awesome promise which precedes it in the same chapter:

"He gives strength to the weary, and to him who lacks might, He increases power." verse 29

The eagle is able to soar when it is caught up in the jet stream of the wind. It cannot soar in its own strength; its innate capacity to fly is maximized by the power which lifts and impels it.

The same thing happens to us when we wait for the caring God to help us. He infuses the tissues of our brains with insight, fills our depleted emotions with His love, fires our wills to discover and do His will, and engenders our bodies with supernatural energy.

Yeats said, "Can one reach God by toil? He gives Himself to the pure in heart. He asks nothing but our attention."

Then we can sing Henry D. Clarke's lovely refrain,
*"He careth for you, He careth for you.
Through sunshine or shadow,
He careth for you."*

Caring Is Spelled P-R-A-Y-I-N-G

Most often we think of caring in terms of action; there is something we must do for a person in order for him or her to know that we really care. That's true, but there is a more powerful expression of caring that comes before action and often clarifies the quality of our specific acts of caring. Being in prayer for another person is profound caring. The Lord has ordained that some of His best gifts are given when we pray for others.

So often we say, "There's nothing I can do except pray." Except pray? When we come to our heavenly Father out of concern for another, all of heaven stops to listen. Our prayers unleash the power of God for a friend or loved one. As we linger in prolonged prayer for a person, we are also given discernment about his or her needs and specific marching orders as to what is maximum for us to do to help.

Right now, in the quiet of your own prayer, spread out before the Lord the concerns you have for the people He's placed on your heart. Surrender the people and the needs to Him. He's listening—be sure of that!—and He will act. The desire to pray is evidence that the answer is waiting.

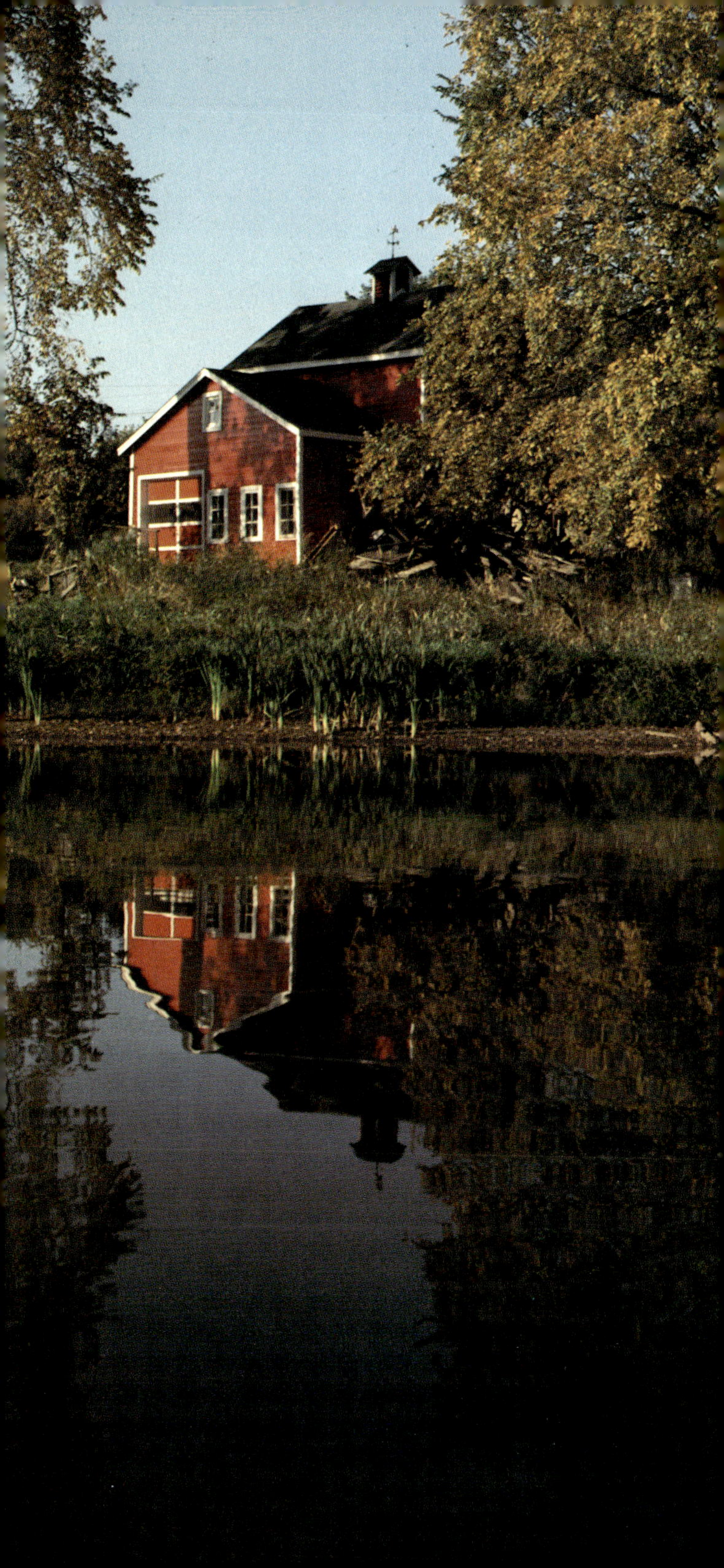

Help From Above

What happened through Annie Johnson Flint was because of what she allowed God to do with what happened to her. She gave the world poems of joy in spite of her physical suffering. Her confidence was in God's care.

*"Got hath not promised
Skies ever blue,
Flower-strewn pathways
All our lives through;
God hath not promised
Sun without rain,
Joy without sorrow,
Peace without pain.*

*"God hath not promised
Smooth roads and wide,
Swift, easy travel
Needing no guide;
God hath not promised
We shall not bear
Many a burden,
Many a care.*

*"But God HATH promised
Strength for the day,
Rest amid labor,
Light for the way;
Grace for the trials,
Help from above,
Unfailing sympathy,
Undying love."*

The Lord Provides for What He Guides!

"Should we feel at times disheartened and discouraged, a simple movement of heart toward God will renew our powers. Whatever He may demand of us, He will give us at the moment the strength and courage that we need."

Francois de Salignac de la Mothe Fenelon

A caring person discovers the joy of being a channel of the Holy Spirit. Inflow and outflow are perfectly matched. We are called to care and are given grace. The decision to care opens the floodgate.

When we surrender our lives to be agents of the Lord's caring in situations and for people, we admit that we do not belong to ourselves. We belong to our Lord and to people who need His love; and with His perfect timing and unlimited resources, He gives us His own Spirit to match the needs. We will be given love, wisdom and the freedom to give ourselves away. The Lord always provides for what He guides!

You Can't Take It Alone!

"Casting all your care upon Him, for He cares for you."

I Peter 5:7, NKJV

When we open ourselves to caring, eventually we have more than we can take alone. All the troubled people, our sick and suffering world, the violence and hatred finally get to us. It is then that we have two alternatives, neither of which seems to work. We either decide that human need is too much to bear, or we build a wall around our hearts to become impervious to the sights and sounds of hurting people.

The third possibility is to realize that we can't take it alone. We were never meant to! Our assurance is not that God will never give us more than we can bear, but that He will never leave us alone to bear the caring in our own strength.

That's why a caring person must also be a praying person. We have not been asked to repeat Calvary by suffering for people, but to claim the love of the cross for people. When we cast our cares on the Lord, we discover what He wants us to do and then are freed to leave the results to Him.

All That There Is of Me

"I will tell you the secret: God has had all that there was of me. There have been men with greater brains than I, even with greater opportunities, but from the day I got the poor...on my heart and caught a vision of what Jesus Christ could do with me and them, on that day I made up my mind that God should have all of William Booth there was. And if there is anything of power...it is because God has had all the adoration of my heart, all the power of my will, and all the influence of my life."

William Booth

That's it!—the equation of a caring person. A vision of the poor, plus what Jesus Christ could do, multiplied by all that there is of us, equals adventuresome living. Who are the poor in your life? the poor in physical and spiritual need? They may be in the slums or in an executive suite. Based on what God has done in your life, what is your vision of what He can do through you? Does He have all of you? That's all He asks.

"God's work done in God's way will never lack God's supplies."

J. Hudson Taylor

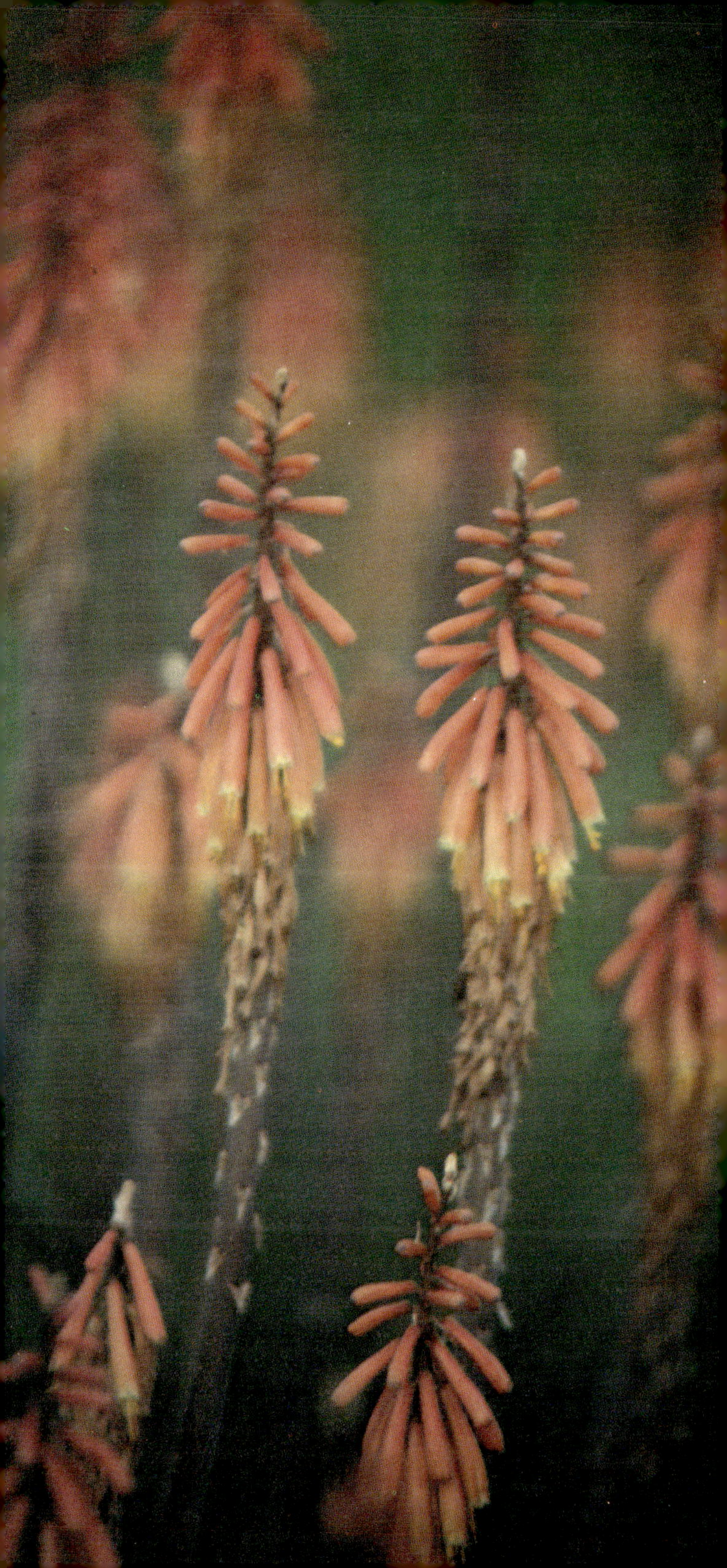

When Nothing Less Will Do

"He will baptize you with the Holy Spirit and fire."

Matthew 3:11, NKJV

The Holy Spirit and fire! John's prophecy was fulfilled on Pentecost.

The fire of the Holy Spirit purifies, produces warmth and galvanizes. When the Lord who is the Spirit takes up residence in us, He burns out the dross of anything which could make us ineffective disciples. As in the centering process of purifying metal, the impurities are brought to the surface and skimmed away.

Then, the sure sign that the Holy Spirit is at work in us is an inclusive, affirming warmth toward others. Lastly, we are galvanized into a unity and oneness with other believers. The gift of profound fellowship occurs. That leaves us with personal questions. Are we on fire? In what ways do we quench, put out or subdue the fire? We need the Holy Spirit when nothing less will do!

"Every time we say, 'I believe in the Holy Spirit,' we mean that we believe that there is a living God able and willing to enter human personality and change it."

J. B. Phillips

"Before Christ sent the Church into the world, He sent the Spirit into the Church. The same order must be observed today."

John R. W. Stott

Help People Come Home

*I*an Maclaren has left an indelible mark in history for his great Scottish stories. One of them is about Lackland Campbell and his daughter, Dora.

Dora left home and became a prodigal daughter. She squandered herself and the gifts of life in self-destructive behavior. She needed to go home but found it difficult because of what she had become.

A letter from her aunt Maggie ends with poignant words of caring. "Dora, your daddy is a grievin' ye. Come home for your own sake. Come home for your daddy's sake. But, Dora, come home most of all for the dear Lord's sake!"

God came in Christ to invite us home. The words of an old hymn articulate the loving, caring invitation. "Softly and tenderly Jesus is calling, Calling for you and for me.... Come home, come home,...come home!"

The purpose of caring for people is to incarnate that appeal. Whatever we do for people is preparatory to helping them to meet Christ, realize the love and forgiveness He offers and come home to Him, to the real persons He meant them to be, and to the abundant life He offers, now and forever. A sure sign that we have come home ourselves is that we want everyone to be "at home" with us in our Father's loving heart.

Here Am I, Send Me!

"My mind is absorbed with the sufferings of man. Since I was twenty-four, there never has been any vagueness in my plans or ideas as to what God's work was for me."

Florence Nightingale

"Then I heard the voice of the Lord, saying, 'Whom shall I send, and who will go for us? Then I said, 'Here am I. Send me!'"

Isaiah 6:8

Isaiah's vision of the Lord resulted in an undeniable call. Life really begins when our experiences of the Lord's glory, love and forgiveness open us to hear the "Whom shall I send?" The world is filled with lonely, worried, anxious, troubled people. Say, "Here am I, send me!" and He will.

The sense of being sent, of being a person under orders, under new management, changes everything. We can work, give ourselves away, become involved in caring, with a winsome freedom. The must becomes a joyous may. When we are called, there is no grim compulsion. The "have-to's" become delights because we are working for the Lord. Then there is no limit to what we are willing to attempt in caring for people and their needs.

Have you been called? Focus your attention on the Lord, the cross, the abundant life He has given you now and the eternal life which death cannot end. Then listen for His call. Say the words in your own soul. "Here am I, Lord—my time, my schedule, my influence, my money, my talents and gifts. Send me!"

Always Beginning Again!

*"I wish that there were some
  wonderful place
In the Land of Beginning Again:
Where all our mistakes and all
  our heartaches
And all of our poor selfish grief
Could be dropped like a shabby
  old coat at the door
And never put on again."*

Louisa Fletcher Tarkington

"From now on, therefore, we regard no one from a human point of view.... Therefore, if any one is in Christ, he is a new creation; the old has passed away, behold, the new has come. All this is from God, who through Christ reconciled us to himself and gave us the ministry of reconciliation...."

II Corinthians 5:16-18, RSV

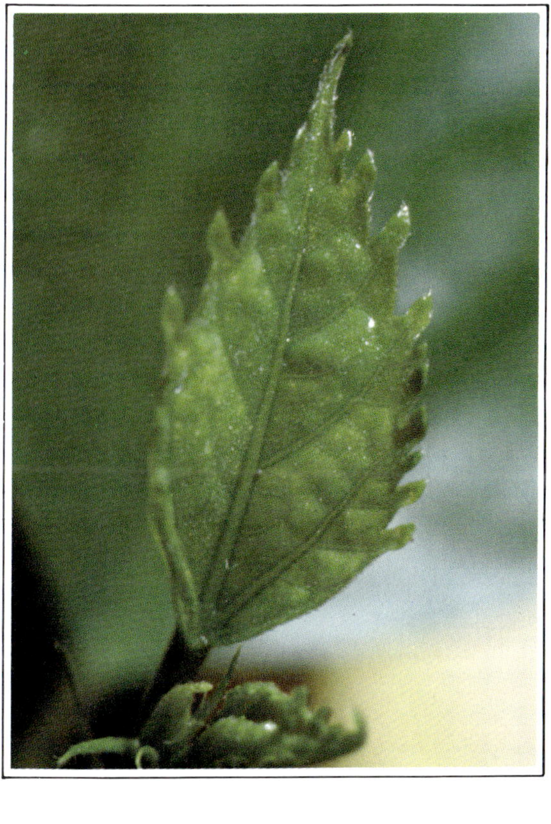

Our lack of caring in the past haunts us. All the missed opportunities flood our minds. All the thoughts, quotes and poetry we have read about caring can be a "quilted" cage locking us up in our remembered neglect—unless today can be a first day in the land of beginning again!

Confession of our "care-lessness" can open us up to the healing of the past. You can become a caring person! Picture what you would be like, filled with Jesus Christ's Spirit, caring as He cared. Hold that image. It will be so by His gift and power.

Photo Credits:
Renee Lee Vaira; pages 32, 53
All other photos by
Koechel/Peterson Design